RAIN 'EM UP

tell me about
FAITH

created by
STEPHEN ELKINS

illustrated by
RUTH ZEGLIN & SIMON TAYLOR-KIELTY

Tyndale House Publishers, Inc.
Carol Stream, Illinois

choo choo
choo choo
choo choo

ALL ABOARD!

All aboard the Gospel train!

Get on Board, Little Children

FIND THIS SONG
on the CD

The gospel train is comin'
The wheels go 'round and 'round
We're training up the children
So they'll be heaven bound

Chorus
Get on board, little children
Get on board, little children
Get on board, little children
There's room for many a-more

Hear that train a-comin'
Comin' down the track
I'll be getting on it
And won't be lookin' back

Repeat chorus

You won't need a penny
To ride this glorious train
Just give your heart to Jesus
And ride away with Him

Repeat chorus

Have you ever wondered what

FAITH is?

welcome to
BIBLE LAND

Yes, I have!
What is **FAITH?**

We're off to
DISCOVERY LAND
to find the answer.

Let's discover what the Bible says about **FAITH.**

1 Mile

DISCOVERY LAND

Some people think  **FAITH**

is believing in yourself and the things you can see.

The Bible says **FAITH** is believing in a God you **cannot** see. Let's find out more about FAITH!

We begin with two little words: "Trust" and "Faith." When you TRUST in something or someone, you BELIEVE they will do what they say. For example, you can trust an airplane will fly but never get on it.

FAITH, however, is putting your trust into action! You show FAITH by getting on the airplane and flying high in the sky! FAITH is putting our trust and belief into action! FAITH always requires action!

· ·

Anyone who doesn't breathe is dead, and faith that doesn't do anything is just as dead! **JAMES 2:26, CEV**

FAITH IS belief in action.

HAVING FAITH an airplane will fly is one thing. But what does it mean to have faith in God? It's more than just trusting that God is real. Faith is putting your belief into action!

Faith in God causes us to do something! We say "yes" to what pleases God, and "no" to what doesn't. Our good works alone do not produce faith. Just the opposite is true: our faith in God always produces good works! So have faith in God.

. . . .

"Have faith in God," Jesus answered. **MARK 11:22, NIV**

EVERYONE HAS FAITH in something. But not everyone has faith in God. When your faith is in Yahweh, Father, it produces a right way of thinking.

You understand who you really are and how things really came to be. You depend on God to be your helper and walk by faith, not by sight! You know He is leading you. You believe He loves you! Faith in God helps us understand the world we live in!

....

By faith we understand that the entire universe was formed at God's command. **HEBREWS 11:3**

FAITH is being CERTAIN!

14

WHEN WE ARE CERTAIN something is true, there is no doubt! As believers, we are certain that the God we cannot see is real. Yet, it was He who made the things we CAN see! He watches over all He created, and He loves His creation.

Our faith isn't just wishful thinking. The Bible says that God's power is clearly seen by the things He has made (Romans 1:20). That's how we can be certain God is real!

. . . .

Now faith is the certainty that what we cannot see exists. **HEBREWS 11:1, ISB**

WHEN WE PUT OUR TRUST into action, that's called faith. We believe by faith that God is our strength. He becomes the most important Person in our life! So we talk to Him each day. We praise Him in word and song!

That kind of faith pleases God! In fact, the Bible says that without faith, it is impossible to please God. Good works alone won't win God's approval. If you really want to please God, show Him your faith!

. . . .

Without faith it is impossible to please God. **HEBREWS 11:6, NIV**

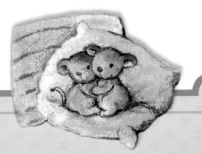

THE HALL OF FAITH

HEBREWS 11 is sometimes called the Great Hall of FAITH. Here we read about great heroes of faith!

Noah was a man of faith. Before it rained, he built an ark! That's real faith! Abraham put his trust into action. He obeyed God by moving his family, and not knowing where he was going!

STORY JUNCTION

Moses put his trust into action! He led God's people out of Egypt to the Promised Land. Put your trust into action!

That's real FAITH!

FIND THIS SONG
on the CD

FAITH IS BEING SURE

Chorus

Faith is being sure of what we hope for
Faith is being certain
Of what we do not see

Faith is saying to the mountain,
"Be moved! Be moved!"
Faith is saying to the mountain,
"Be moved! Be moved!"

Repeat Chorus

**ADAPTED FROM
HEBREWS 11:1, NIV**
Words & music by Stephen Elkins

BRIDGE OF SONG

WHAT HAVE WE LEARNED ABOUT FAITH?

(answers at bottom of page)

1. Our faith is in _____.

2. Faith is acting on what you _____.

3. Faith brings _____.

4. Faith is being _____.

5. Faith pleases _____.

LEARNING STATION

1. God, 2. believe, 3. understanding, 4. certain, 5. God.

Are you ready to put **YOUR FAITH** in **GOD** above?

Are you ready to **TURN YOUR TRUST INTO FAITH** by acting on what you believe?

Do you believe that **FAITH BRINGS UNDERSTANDING?**

Are you ready to **PLEASE GOD** by exercising your faith?

Then you are ready to **WALK BY FAITH AND NOT BY SIGHT!**

DECISION DEPOT

LORD, hear us when we PRAY:

DEAR YAHWEH FATHER,

I love You and thank You for giving me a measure of faith. I want my faith to please You. I trust You with all my heart, and I want to put my trust into action.

Show me what to do, Lord. Lead me in the path you want me to go. Give me understanding so that I can better walk by faith and not by sight. And let my faith produce good works that please You. **This I ask in Jesus' name, Amen!**

PRAYER PLACE

TRAIN UP A CHILD

FIND THIS SONG on the CD

Train up, train up,
Train up a child in the way he should go.
Train up, train up,
Train up a child in the way she should go.
And when they are older
They will not depart from it.

**ADAPTED FROM
PROVERBS 22:6**

Words & music by Stephen Elkins

I know the LORD must love all this great singing!

And He loves you, too!

Last stop! Good-bye, everybody. *See you next time when once again we'll choo-choo away aboard the Gospel train and discover all that God has for us!*